NATURE *takes over*

THE DESIGNS OF BILL HARPER

Bill J. Harper, AIFD, AAF, FAM, is one of the floral industry's most accomplished designers, educators, consultants and lecturers. His love and appreciation of nature was cultivated on his family's farm in rural Missouri, where he lives to this day.

Bill's career has placed him in many roles, including floral artist and visual merchandiser. His designs have been featured in magazines and books, both nationally and internationally, over the past three decades. He is one of six American designers featured in the millennium edition of *World Flower Artists 2* (2000), and he has been a frequent contributor to *Florists' Review* magazine for more than 25 years.

As a teacher, Bill has traveled extensively throughout the United States, Europe and Asia conducting schools, workshops and exhibitions. As a product-development consultant, he has traveled to China, making significant contributions in the innovation of permanent botanicals, floral décor and accessories.

BIOGRAPHY

Bill was inducted into the American Institute of Floral Designers (AIFD) in 1977. Since then, he has served the organization in many ways including national president (1991-1992), membership chair (1984-1988) and National Symposium co-chair (1984, 2003, 2009). In 1996, Bill was presented the Distinguished Service Award to AIFD and honored as a fellow of the organization. Bill is also a member of the American Academy of Floriculture (AAF) and the Floral Academy of Missouri (FAM).

Additional honors include designing at the White House and for three presidential inaugurations as well as for the rededication of the Statue of Liberty (1986). Bill also was the first runner-up in the 1974 FTD America's Cup design competition.

Bill's extensive experience and design acumen have been enhanced by his love of art and horticulture. Tirelessly inquisitive, Bill sees ordinary objects in the most extraordinary ways. Innovation is his trademark.

FOREWORD

Bill Harper approaches flowers with unparalleled passion and wondrous clarity of vision. For the enthusiast, his arranging is playful and entertaining. For the professional, his process is awe inspiring, as each flower, leaf, branch and blade of grass is efficiently positioned without hesitation or second guessing. When he is finished, the result is perfection from every angle.

Bill's expansive knowledge of floral design, theory and history, combined with his straightforward application of the elements and principles of art, establishes a well-researched foundation for each project he approaches. But it's his enthusiasm for nature that makes the arrangements come to life with an exuberance that is usually found only in nature itself.

The countless hours Bill has spent tending his garden and observing how plants grow on his family farm have awarded him a sensitivity rarely found in a floral designer. Yet at the core of his personality, Bill is a teacher, and it's the kind and generous way he shares his abilities and knowledge that makes him so loved and respected by his peers in the floral community.

As I talked with Bill about each design he created for this book, he frequently ended his descriptions with the same conclusion, saying, "Nature took over." For Bill, this is how it really happens. No design is finished without "a certain measure of undisciplined expression coexisting with more controlled form and line."

Bill's creations are collaborations with nature. They are free from pretension and over-calculation and are filled with amazing sensitivity for the materials.

TALMAGE MCLAURIN, AIFD
Publisher, Florists' Review Enterprises

GARDEN

ASIAN

PRAIRIE

MODERN

"All of the elements and principles for art and design are found in nature. Nature is our greatest teacher."

Bill Harper still tends to plantings that his great-grandmother started in the garden of his family homestead, now spanning five generations. This farm in rural Missouri where Bill resides is where he, as a child, fell in love with nature and learned that there is an art to its cultivation. Though his travels have taken him to gardens around the world, Bill always returns in body and spirit to the uncontrolled elegance of his country garden for inspiration and rejuvenation.

GARDEN

Honored here, in an antique hand-painted vase, the rose maintains its rightful status as grande dame of the garden. The vase features 'Anna' and 'Harmony' varieties while a low marbled-glass bowl displays a hand-tied cluster accented by orbiting vines clipped from one of the dozens of climbing bushes in Bill's garden.

Hand-carved angels from Santa Fe are entwined
with sprawling deciduous huckleberry vines.
A feeling of otherworldliness
inhabits the fragrant cascades of 'Virginia' and 'Princess'
roses, lilies-of-the-valley, *Gardenias*, *Hydrangeas*, curly
dock and reed grass while maidenhair vines form
organic halos for the musical trio.

DESIGN TIP Foam-cage wedding bouquet holders are
used to hold the flowers in place. Large and heavy-stemmed
materials are secured into the holders by dipping the stems
into waterproof floral adhesive just prior to insertion.

Bill loves to show the entire flower, from stem to leaf to blossom.

These exposed clusters of *Gerberas*, *Hydrangeas*, *Scabiosas*, *Salvias*, *Coleus*, basil, dusty miller and steel grass celebrate the relationship between the framework of stems and the flowers they support. A perfect accent for casual entertaining, these garden components are enhanced with the playful flicker of candlelight reflecting in the glass.

DESIGN TIP Steel grass is submerged in the largest vase, providing a clean and attractive framework of stems into which additional stems are arranged.

An antique store treasure that never made it to the upholsterer serves as the **architectural background for this garden riot** of *Delphiniums, Ranunculuses,* sweet Williams, Queen Anne's lace, bachelor's buttons, blue lace flowers, coral bells, lavender, *Kalanchoe, Sedum,* prairie grasses and asparagus spears. The distressed finish of the chair harmonizes perfectly with Bill's overgrown garden.

DESIGN TIP Bill replaced the cushion to this chair with a tray filled with moss-covered floral foam, into which he arranged the botanical materials.

Bill is a self-proclaimed Anglophile, and nothing could be more illustrative of this than his **very Victorian formal dining room,** where, central to the ornamentation, is a resplendent classic vase arrangement comprising 'Versilia' roses, *Sedum*, pomegranate branches, snowberries and *Crocosmia* pods.

DESIGN TIP After arranging flowers directly into water, Bill always removes the arrangement, holding the stems in hand, to rinse the vase and refill it with fresh water treated with flower food.

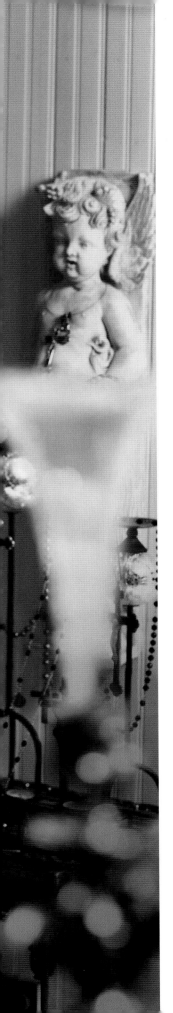

The cloche — which is the French word for "bell" — was designed to **protect delicate plants from frost and wind while promoting the germination** of seedlings, much like a small contained greenhouse. Here, the garden staple is used with a touch of irony, delaying the monarch's migratory obligation. A ring of orange-hued roses, *Gerberas*, *Zinnias*, miniature callas and *Lantana* pair with green bear grass, geranium leaves and *Hypericum* to match the colors of the painted feather butterflies.

DESIGN TIP For the base of this design, an inexpensive plastic tray is covered with fresh *Galax* leaves, which are attached with spray floral adhesive.

Bill's **English-country guest bedroom** hosts a welcoming mix of 'Versilia' roses, lilies-of-the-valley, snowberries, stars-of-Bethlehem, *Coleus*, dusty miller, variegated English ivy, juniper and pine perched atop an antique iron candlestick.

DESIGN TIP To create the base for this design, Bill attached a small bowl, filled with floral foam, to the candlestick with florist's clay.

Rosemary and roses are the perfect marriage of garden fragrances. A classic garland of the herb, shaped into a wreath, hangs gently from the edge of a French-inspired compote of tulips, *Ranunculuses* and roses. With a nod to the garden's circle of life, selected rose centers are removed, representing a garden's ephemeral qualities.

DESIGN TIP To aid in fashioning the rosemary into a wreath shape, each sprig is bound with a gentle wrapping of bullion wire.

What distinguishes this magnificent arrangement from a typical mass design is the dimension that is added when vines, grasses and elongated stems break free from the compact form and show their character and personality. Bringing nature's sprawling tendencies indoors, a mix of French tulips, *Viburnums*, *Celosia*, roses, oak-leaf *Hydrangeas*, blooming *Clematis* vines and poppy pods does justice to the ornate Italian terra-cotta urn.

DESIGN TIP Arrange the tighter mass of materials in the bouquet first, then follow with elongated stems of grasses, vines and slender flowers and buds to add an airy outer layer of materials.

Always holding fragile surprises is how Bill remembers finding nests in the farm meadows as a child. Here, his favorite messenger of spring is handcrafted from mosses and honeysuckle vines to be safely tucked into a thicket of blue hyacinths, *Agapanthuses*, *Eryngiums* and *Trachelium*.

DESIGN TIP Faux bird's nests are easily crafted by wrapping strands of vine, bits of moss and even straw in a circular motion while mixing in a few pieces of florist's wire covered in brown stem wrap to hold it all in place.

17

The possibilities for design are endless, but flexible materials make the opportunity for variation even more exciting. Bill says, of the versatile pussy willows,

"I like to see if I can manipulate them as well as nature grows them."

18

Here are three variations on a theme, each combining the willows with fragrant blue hyacinths, bear grass and butterflies. From fluid loops and curls that frame the hyacinths to a strong vertical column that adds architectural stature to a swirling compacted nest formation, the line and movement of the willows in each arrangement is rerouted with a fresh perspective.

DESIGN TIP When in season, pussy willows are extremely pliable and can be shaped easily. Avoid using dried willows when planning a design that requires manipulation of the stems.

As a child, Bill developed such a fascination for the chore of doing laundry that his father built him his own low-to-the-ground clothesline, so he could pretend to hang the wash. So it's never a surprise to see clothespins show up in his arrangements. Here, they cleverly hold a retro seed packet of perennials onto a glass cube container filled with *Campanulas*, *Delphiniums*, *Gerberas*, 'Gracia' spray roses, 'Vermeer' Asiatic lilies, *Kalanchoe* 'Calandiva' blossoms, lily grass and bear grass.

DESIGN TIP Miniature wooden clothespins can be found at most craft stores and then custom-colored with floral spray paint.

Featuring a stately fowl selected from Bill's mother's collection of more than 30 roosters and sitting on a tile-topped sideboard that was crafted by his father in the 1940s, this buffet setting is a **holiday tradition at the Harper farm.** *Hydrangeas*, *Cotoneaster*, dill, rosemary, sage, Osage oranges, thorn apples, gourds, artichokes, pomegranates, leeks, apples, lemons, broomcorn, quaking grass, tickle grass and fir compose the mounded base while dried grasses harvested from the pastures fan out to provide a backdrop for the carving station.

DESIGN TIP To hold heavy fruits and vegetables in the floral foam, insert six-inch wood picks into the backsides of the items, and then arrange them into the foam.

Thanksgiving memories of a successful year on the farm culminated with
a celebration of the good harvest.
Bill's mother would place branches of turning leaves and gathered gourds in the windows. This contemporary "gathering basket" is actually a copper mining pan pavéd with groupings of bicolor 'Fashion' roses, *Gerberas*, gourds and croton leaves.

DESIGN TIP To add texture and interest to this design, Bill added pieces of folded copper netting between the groupings of botanicals.

A hushed moment of thanksgiving is rewarded with rays of golden sunlight filtering through stained-glass windows onto a matched pair of liturgical altar arrangements showcasing garden roses, *Gerberas*, parrot tulips and fall foliages.

DESIGN TIP When designing in altar vases, always use a hard plastic liner for the florals to avoid leaking and damaging irreplaceable furnishings.

23

Working with natural forms requires an appreciation for the irregularity found in nature. The casual way the materials in this transparent glass urn are collected **celebrates a freedom from conformity** that includes a centrally placed *Gerbera* that is missing petals. *Delphiniums*, *Hydrangeas*, spray roses, stocks, *Campanulas*, *Genista* and lily grass complete the lush composition.

DESIGN TIP When the opening of a container, like the one on this glass urn, is too wide to hold the stems upright, create a grid across the opening with clear waterproof floral tape, dividing it into smaller openings for positioning stems.

The pieces in Bill's collection of blue porcelain are souvenirs from his travels to England, Scotland, Holland and Japan. Blended in a cross-cultural menagerie, they are harmoniously displayed in his kitchen and find a prominence during the holidays, when Bill treats himself to one of his favorite flowers — lilies-of-the-valley. Here, the diminutive blossoms are arranged with *Hydrangeas*, chinaberries, blue plums, apples, privet berries, *Eucalyptus*, *Artemisia*, *Coleus* and geranium foliage, sage and thyme in a striking combination of blue and green hues.

DESIGN TIP Delicate stems, like lilies-of-the-valley, are often too fragile to insert into floral foam. Instead, place these stems into water tubes, and insert the tubes into the foam.

Bill's garden designs are **a dichotomy of cultivated order and natural disarray.** This example features a wicker basket that was seemingly abandoned in the garden and subsequently deconstructed by an untamed gang of wildflowers. Sweet Williams, Queen Anne's lace, *Gerberas*, *Ixias*, *Scabiosas*, globe amaranths and pepper grass join forces to reclaim the discarded basket as their own.

DESIGN TIP   Bill began this design with an inexpensive wicker basket that he disassembled and lined with a second container, which is filled with floral foam to hold the flower stems in place.

True symmetry is rarely found in nature, yet it's the standard of Western architecture. So when natural elements are mixed with classic icons like this garden urn, an interesting contrast can be achieved with asymmetrical placements of materials. This balancing act combines a traditional Romanesque mound of blushing roses and *Ranunculuses* arranged off-center and counterbalanced with a dynamic swirl of honeysuckle vines and English ivy.

DESIGN TIP Begin this design by wrapping the lip of a floral-foam-filled urn with honeysuckle vine and securing it in place with sturdy hairpin-shaped wires that sink deep into the foam. Then thread strands of ivy through the vine, and finish with a mounded mass of florals.

A New Orleans-style courtyard garden inspired this design that displays maximum lushness in minimal space. The weathered tin urn is elevated on stacked plastic trays covered with salal leaves. *Viburnums*; *Hydrangeas*; *Hypericum* berries; *Lantana* pods; and salal, *Hosta*, *Coleus*, geranium, basil, mint and lamb's-ears foliages complete the Big Easy ensemble.

DESIGN TIP Two cost-effective plastic trays, stacked and covered with salal leaves, are used as a base for this design. The bottom tray is inverted to add height to the urn while the second is filled with floral foam to hold the urn and the base of foliage.

A combination of fresh and dried
botanicals tells a transseasonal story.
The contrast of textures
points this vase's
mood toward autumn
and concedes to the impending
winter with unexpected violet tones.
Ornamental kale, late-blooming
Anemones, ink-blue privet berries
and millet compose the ensemble.

DESIGN TIP Wrap the stems of
dried grasses with waterproof tape
when arranging them into water to
prevent them from disintegrating.

Transitioning from winter
to spring, a verdant carpet of
green mosses mixed with fuzzy,
mosslike *Dianthuses* sets
a stage for forcing the season.
Tiny daffodils
are warmed and
protected by
a bell-shaped
cloche while on
the outside, barren winter
branches wait patiently to bud.

DESIGN TIP The daffodils in this design began as potted bulbs from which the soil is washed, and the roots are nestled into floral foam with some positioning help from sturdy hairpin-shaped wires.

Clipped from a cutting garden and paired with romantic paper greetings, this arrangement, in a modern vase, includes a giftable rooting stock of roses and *Ranunculuses.* An armature of salal stems holds the blossoms in place. Bill reminds that gifts from the garden should be followed by a return favor but never with a thank-you. Superstition holds that garden thank-yous are bad luck, and it's the generosity of nature for which gratitude is reserved.

DESIGN TIP Floral graphics can be cut from wrapping paper and greeting cards and secured to containers with spray floral adhesive.

Swirling honeysuckle vines hide the mechanics
of this explosion of color that resembles
a rowdy English chintz fabric.
'Joey' garden roses, 'Timeless' and 'Orange Unique'
hybrid tea roses, *Campanulas*, blue lace flowers,
hyacinths, *Alliums*, *Viburnums*, *Skimmia* and blue
lepto create the glowing graphic garden.

DESIGN TIP A low plastic tray created for casket designs can
be used for centerpiece arrangements when the materials will
extend to the surface of the table and conceal the container.

"If there is any form of design
that is truly, truly
in tune with nature,
it has to be Asian."

When Bill Harper first traveled to Japan, it was to teach Western design, but along the way he may have learned as much as he taught. Bill is quick to point out that he has no formal training in ikebana, yet he is compelled to interpret the stylings at which he has marveled on his countless visits.

In fact, many of Bill's personal design philosophies are so closely related to Eastern floral design that it's difficult to sort them out. Both philosophies **respect every flower and recognize the symbolism of the materials.** And in both styles of design, every composition tells a story—one that brings us all to a greater appreciation of nature.

ASIAN

Bill acquired this 18th-century usubata, a traditional vase for classical ikebana arrangements, from an antique dealer in Kurashiki, Japan. Often cast in bronze, these heavyweighted containers are favorite choices for the traditional and elaborate Rikka-style arrangements. Bill's interpretive design, however, favors more modern applications of Seika or contemporary freestyle, celebrating the stretching lines of pear branches and lily grass combined with 'Apricot Parrot' tulips, *Ranunculuses* and *Ornithogalums*.

Representing a Zen garden, the nest of lacquered trays is precisely arranged, reflecting the sense of orderly precision that is common throughout most aspects of Japanese culture. *Gerberas* and *Ranunculuses* emerge from a courtyard of gravel and are followed by subsequent rows of *Hypericum* berries, stacked salal leaves and red dogwood branches. Dynamic lines of lily grass and deciduous branches artfully disrupt the order.

DESIGN TIP The multiple edges visible in the row of salal leaves are achieved by folding each leaf in half lengthwise so that two edges are visible instead of one. Stapling several folded leaves together helps keep the edges in alignment.

The intricately woven silk textiles used to make the national costume of Japan, **the kimono,** and the belt, or obi, that wraps it are interpreted in a collage of floral materials including *Hydrangea* florets, *Anthuriums,* japhette orchids, larkspurs, *Nerines*, *Eryngiums*, spray roses and bear grass.

DESIGN TIP The disc-shaped base of this collage is a round piece of cardboard covered with foliages and flat florets, which are secured with spray floral adhesive. The three-dimensional materials are arranged into a foam-cage wedding bouquet holder.

Influenced by the Japanese *Tsukiyama* garden (hill garden), this collection of *Lisianthuses*, *Agapanthuses*, lily grass and pussy willows creates a miniature landscape that mimics hills, stones, trees, flowers, bridges and paths in a cultivated garden.

DESIGN TIP Individual florets from stems of *Agapanthuses* are removed and clustered to form a lush ground cover.

Symbolizing a *Chaniwa* garden that is built for the tea ceremony (*Sado*), and accommodates the teahouse *(chashitsu)*, these terraced arrangements feature the typical stepping stones that lead toward the teahouse where *Sado* is performed. *Ranunculuses*, grasses and branches complete the garden design. The repetition of the stepping stones and the progression of crossing blades of lily grass create visual movement (rhythm) through the designs that bridges the gap between the two containers.

Rice bowls with a floral twist prove that novelty flower designs can be modern and relevant.

Nurturing both the soul and the spirit, along with the body, the focus of Asian food is presentation first.

Mosslike Dianthuses, Hypericum berries, chrysanthemum petals, geranium leaves and lily grass supply these clever floral entrées.

DESIGN TIP Interesting and often inexpensive containers used for dining or the preparation of food are easily accessible options for displaying flowers.

Anemones, variegated lily grass and lamb's-ears foliage are combined with collected vines and grasses in an arrangement that mirrors nature at water's edge. This strict natural design style mimics arrangements made for tea ceremonies, where, in sharp contrast to stylized ikebana, the arrangements are designed with strict aesthetic simplicity. **Only 10 seconds are allowed for the gathering and placement of flowers for tea ceremonies,** so all bending, shaping and human intervention is eliminated, and the materials are presented in their original and natural state.

DESIGN TIP Arrangements of this genre require calculated thought when selecting materials. Choose only botanicals that naturally coexist.

Water features are a mainstay of Zen gardens,
especially in *Karesansui* gardens (rock gardens), where natural land-
scapes are presented in an abstract way. For this meditative
composition of lily grass and floating waxflower blossoms, Bill placed
an 18th-century ceramic bowl he sourced on the island of Shikoku in
the center to represent an elegant reflecting pool.

DESIGN TIP The slightly tilted placement of the
ceramic bowl in the tray of gravel promotes a more
organic and natural feeling to the overall composition.

43

Wabi-sabi, sometimes called Japanese rustic design, is an art form that, like nature, seeks to maintain a balance between growth and decay. Great beauty is found and celebrated in the character of aging and imperfect objects. We can see those tenets represented here, in a story of three ceramic pots that follows the stages of life from youth to old age, as two *Gerberas* start near to the earth, mature by reaching out and stretching, and, finally, end their life by dropping the petals that encumber.

DESIGN TIP Don't discard materials that seem, at first, imperfect or damaged by age. Consider how they can be displayed so that the beauty of their character can be appreciated.

Moon gates, originating in China, were first found in the gardens of the country's nobility.

These circular gateways in walls were placed in the gardens as pedestrian passageways, making an introduction to the garden more inviting. Bill's version of the moon gate shows the moon in three stages, using smooth stones, croton leaves and red dogwood twigs to enhance the view.

DESIGN TIP   The red dogwood twigs in this design are more than visual enhancements. Placed tightly into the bowls, they gently wedge the Gerberas and croton leaves into position. The Japanese call this technique of using twigs or branches to support the placement of materials hana-kubari (or kubari).

45

This modern foliage design utilizes variegated *Aspidistra* leaves to create the look of swirling water.

Alchemilla blossoms, date pods, lily grass and salal stems fill the remainder of the container, creating an interesting potpourri of texture.

DESIGN TIP To create the swirl of *Aspidistra* leaves, Bill first cut each leaf into two pieces – cutting close to and discarding the stiff spines. Next, he covered an inverted paint can lid with a leaf, using spray floral adhesive. He then coiled leaves inside the lid. More leaves, which are held in place with occasional drops of waterproof floral adhesive, continue the swirl outside the lid.

This grouping of containers reminds Bill of the terraced gardens in Japan. Both garden enthusiastic and space challenged, the Japanese use a variety of support elements to facilitate these multilevel plantings. Here, three simple twig containers and an elaborate stacked-twig lattice column create multiple opportunities for this display of variegated *Aspidistra* leaves, *Ranunculuses*, *Hydrangeas*, grasses and branches. A central medallion, made from a *Galax*-leaf-covered disk, a bundle of twigs and a ring of copper wire, punctuates the look.

DESIGN TIP A large display with just a few materials can be achieved by displaying multiple simple designs, created in several containers, together as a single unit.

These uniquely decorated tilelike trays are reminiscent of variations on the same wood block pattern.

Spray roses, Hypericum, Equisetum, bear grass, red huckleberry foliage, red dogwood branches, marbles and copper wire are employed to fabricate these intricately detailed designs. They will look as interesting when they have dried as they do as fresh floral art pieces.

DESIGN TIP These presentations are contained within affordable plastic trays covered with Galax leaves that are attached with spray floral adhesive. Each design begins with a floral foam ring that is secured into the center of the tray with florist's clay.

Paper and wire are common media used in the Japanese art of origami. This grouping, with its nod to the art form, is created with a celebration in mind. Red, the color of celebration, and flickering candles dominate the collection that features fresh *Anthuriums* supported on a weaving of fern fronds and dried pimentina.

DESIGN TIP The origami sticks are made on inexpensive wooden skewers found in any grocery store and custom-colored with floral paint.

In the Tibetan Buddhist tradition,

spinning a "prayer wheel," called a "mani chho-khor," is said to have the same effect as reciting prayers orally. Authentic prayer wheels are made from metal, wood, stone and leather, and the mantra (prayer) "Om Mani Padme Hum" is written in Sanskrit on the outside, but this interpretive incarnation is fashioned from roses wrapped with Aspidistra leaves. A loose wrapping and medallions of gold bullion wire are incorporated in place of the mantra.

DESIGN TIP This "prayer wheel" can double as a wedding bouquet for an Asian-themed nuptial event. The form is created using a foam-filled designer tray as the base, with a handle repurposed from a bouquet holder glued to the underside of the tray.

In most typical homes in Asia, flowers are a part of the décor, but they carry richer traditions and greater symbolism than in the West. **Learning to arrange flowers properly is considered as much an every-day skill as a professional one.** This arrangement shows an interpretation of the right-hand pattern for a standard Seika-style design, with the *shin* (heaven) being the tall piece of red dogwood, *soe* (man) being the position held by the *Anthurium*, and the geranium leaves as the *tai* (earth), completing the three points of an asymmetrical triangle.

DESIGN TIP Adding ornamentation to a composition of this nature should be executed with great subtlety. Bill used a simple bundle of red dogwood twigs and a coil of thin copper wires to avoid overpowering the stronger elements of the design.

Late evening in a Japanese garden, with lengthening shadows and all colors turning to gray,
is how Bill describes the understatement of these designs.
Simplified with an absence of color, this pair of garden pots
feature fern shoots, lotus pods and waxflowers and find their
magic in the subtleties and silhouettes of the gloaming.

DESIGN TIP   To cover the exposed surfaces of the floral foam
inside the pots, Bill positioned leftover pieces of the fern shoots
side by side to create a natural "flooring" that resembles bamboo. The shoots are held in place with hairpin-shaped wires.

For Bill, connecting with Asian culture has strongly influenced his approach to floral design. The bridge between Eastern and Western aesthetics is beautifully represented in a composition that joins the *Cymbidium* orchids and *Dahlias* (symbolic of gratitude) with connecting placements of lily grass and *Ranunculus* buds.

DESIGN TIP Inexpensive aquarium gravel is an efficient and attractive material with which to cover exposed floral foam.

55

The garden lantern, an everyday element in Japan, is elevated to a position of greater importance in this pair of lacquerlike trays. Celebrating the simple things is a way of life in Japanese culture. Here, in one tray, lush garden botanicals, including *Zinnias*, *Gerberas*, miniature callas, *Coleus* and geranium leaves, and quaking and steel grasses, flank a pathway of smooth garden stones that lead to the second tray holding a celebration of tiny votive candles arranged in an orderly Zen-like manner.

DESIGN TIP A "mulch" of finely cut steel grass camouflages a layer of saturated floral foam that holds the flowers securely and provides an adequate water source.

Japanese rooftop gardens contrast
disciplined and restrained architecture with the sprawling and
dynamic lines of cultivated plants.
These two "rooftop" miniatures begin with high-rise
and low-rise containers featuring flat rims that
extend over the sides of the vessels. Carnations,
Cymbidium orchids, hanging *Amaranthus*,
Trachelium, lily grass and deciduous huckleberry
branches make for colorful landscaping.

DESIGN TIP Horizontal rows of river cane
arranged at the base of the lower design extends the
architectural lines of the containers and provides a
lower level that adds depth to the composition.

"The prairie gives me **endless space, a limitless sky and a community of plants** and animals that spark my creativity."

Bill Harper grew up on the edge of the prairie. Its open space, subtle rolling horizons and seas of grasses are as much a part of his personality as his family ties to the Native Americans who first inhabited the land. These influences, apparent in his aesthetic, inspire a love and respect for the prairie that is tempered with concern for this endangered ecosystem, 95 percent of which has been destroyed. Bill's prairie-style designs are his most emotional creations, rich with the grandeur of the setting and filled with hope that man and nature will again, one day, successfully coexist.

PRAIRIE

Bill's backyard water feature is the perfect venue for a collection of native grasses. The cement spheres, cast in plastic beer containers, host a water fountain in which birds happily drink and bathe. Here, converted into floral vases, the fountain displays indigenous materials from the prairie including Solomon's-seal, cypress grass, buffalo grass, sour dock, wild ferns and naturally shed deer antlers paired with commercially grown *Sarracenias.*

The first signs of spring are seen in this carryall basket containing jonquils that have popped through winter-weary grasses. Monarch butterflies, symbols of hope and freedom, remind Bill of the magical migrations that he saw as a child, when thousands of butterflies briefly visited the farm.

DESIGN TIP The faux, painted-feather butterflies are easily attached directly to stems and branches by clipping away their wire stems and securing them with a drop of hot glue.

The grasshopper, a crop liability for the family farm, was also a partner to one of Bill's childhood pastimes — when he could catch them. Here the green grasshopper hosts a more contemporary display of jonquils.

DESIGN TIP Holding stems together in a decorative way, these grasshoppers are actually napkin rings that are slipped around the clusters of jonquils and bear grass.

Modest flowers and weathered leaves inhabit this utilitarian clay container that might have been **discarded from a wagon train by early settlers.** Late-summer conditions are responsible for the parched grasses and the fallen petals of the emblematic Midwestern sunflowers. Bold-colored geranium leaves and velvety lamb's-ears leaves complete the collection.

DESIGN TIP Bill removed petals from one sunflower to allow this design to tell a story about the beauty of nature at its less-than-perfect stage.

An abandoned fence-row of a prairie homestead is left to the wills of nature, as indigenous materials mix with domesticated plants.

Liatrises, Gerberas, Queen Anne's lace, blue lace flowers, daisy spray chrysanthemums, 'Monte Cassino' *Asters*, mullein leaves, gorse, koala fern, pepper grass and asparagus spears join forces in nature's re-beautification project.

DESIGN TIP This design is built around wooden fencing that has been deconstructed and faux-painted to look old and broken down.

The parallels between the music and artwork of Native American and Asian cultures have long fascinated Bill. Here, he pairs hawk feathers and bark (found prairie objects) with native grasses, pimentina, pear branches and *Eryngiums* in a way that

captures the peaceful serenity and sensibilities of both cultural expressions.

DESIGN TIP Incorporating sculptural elements, like this wooden bird finial, helps make abstract designs more relevant and meaningful to the observer.

Sophisticated elements, like *Stephanotises,* silver-plated pine cones and an elegantly weathered finial, combine with more common elements, like shed deer antlers, dried pine cones, pine branches and an orb covered in lamb's-ears and *Coleus* leaves, in this

European-inspired assemblage.

DESIGN TIP Silver-colored decorative wires and sprinkles of faux snow are used to highlight this frost-kissed collection of found objects.

The dynamics of the windblown prairie

are represented in the angles of dramatically positioned dried grasses and feathers in this abstract collection that includes pine cones, millet, shed deer antlers, fern shoots and barren branches. Central to the collection is an unusual stone that Bill picked up by a stream in southern Missouri. Upon closer inspection, he realized, from the obvious wear of rawhide bindings, that this rock had been used as a primitive tool or weapon by a Native American and, just possibly, an ancestor.

DESIGN TIP Bill incorporated the vase into this design by extending materials below the lip of the cylinder and by attaching elements onto its surface.

Only birds can make nests better than Bill; in fact, he might give some a little competition. This bird's nest, made from vines and tickle grass, is the perfect complement to the abstract tapestry that is formed under glass and brimming with treasures Bill has collected on nature walks (opposite page). They include grasses, feathers, pine cones and fungus from a black locust tree.

DESIGN TIP Bill's secret to creating natural-looking yet securely constructed nests is bullion wire. He discretely incorporates the wire by wrapping it around a few of the vines, adding a pliable stiffness to the bundle. He also uses the wire to connect materials as he wraps them in circular formation.

This snow-dusted formal-linear
arrangement comprises bald-
cypress seed pods, lamb's-ears
foliage, dusty miller, cone-laden
pine branches, cascading rosary
vine and a curling castor-bean
leaf that was hit by frost,
marking a transi-
tion from autumn
into winter.

DESIGN TIP A rusted disc plate from a tractor and a discarded fence finial, both repurposed farm antiques, supply
quintessential elements that add distinction to this design
and provide inspiration for using other salvaged elements

Materials from the prairie garden combine with roses and *Hydrangeas* to pavé this polished aluminum bowl with **a study in textural contrast.** Shed deer antlers break the calmness of the composition.

DESIGN TIP Adding an element of surprise to the composition, like these deer antlers, creates interest and gives the design the necessary flair that makes it special.

71

DESIGN TIP The stunning wreath that creates one of the focal points is a plastic-foam form covered with lamb's-ears and *Coleus* leaves, adhered with spray floral adhesive. Bindings of bullion wire accent the form.

An elegant old home on the prairie, with elements of both sophistication and neglect, were in mind when Bill designed these two distinctive urn arrangements. Native prairie botanicals contrast with the classic-shaped containers, elegant finials, crystal orbs, chandelier crystals from London's historic Covent Garden and a timeless wreath covered with foliages. Botanical elements include roses, false spiraea, dusty miller, Coleus foliage, flat cedar and rosary vine.

Impressions of water from this thick, blue glass vase provide a calming contrast to the earthy mix of 'Virginia' roses, ornamental kale and an artichoke combined with buckskin-colored sycamore leaves, vines and clusters of black privet berries.

DESIGN TIP   The combination of fresh and dried materials in a single composition brings a textural contrast that is particularly effective in autumn and winter presentations.

The spontaneous art created by a fallen pine branch is celebrated in these component designs. Bill customized the contemporary vases with bark, lamb's-ears foliage and vine wrappings to make them relevant to the botanicals they contain, and the fallen pine branches combine with sky-blue and green *Eryngiums*, reflecting the rich azure hue of the winter sky.

DESIGN TIP The leaves and bark on the slick-surfaced vases are secured with waterproof floral adhesive. Additional materials, including the vines and branches, are held in place with bullion wire.

A collection box of treasures
from the prairie creates a
three-dimensional storybook,
with each element adding a new chapter to
the intriguing tome. Feathers, birch bark,
Magnolia leaves, fern fronds, pine cones, red
dogwood branches, copper wire and polished
stones are included.

DESIGN TIP   To give the collection more sta-
bility, the branches and bark are tightly wedged
into the tray first. The remaining materials are
tucked between those supporting elements.

The intensely colorful sunsets in the prairie sky are popular themes for Midwestern artists. **Bill's tribute to a spectacular autumn sky** full of warm colors includes a pumpkin and a pear, peach roses, *Pyracantha* berries, frost-bronzed foliages and feathers.

DESIGN TIP Before arranging ivy vines that are harvested from a plant into either floral foam or water, hydrate them thoroughly by soaking them in room-temperature water overnight.

Fire is common on the unplowed prairies; in fact, the prairies rely on fires for healthy rejuvenation of the soil. These arrangements depict fire, smoke, wind and lightning that are part of turning what seems, at first, an adversity into an advantage. Geranium foliage, *Gerberas*, native grasses, feathers and branches embody the composition.

DESIGN TIP Choosing a vessel that represents the message of a design is as important as choosing the appropriate elements in the arrangement. These containers aptly represent the smoking prairie in the colors of the earth and sky.

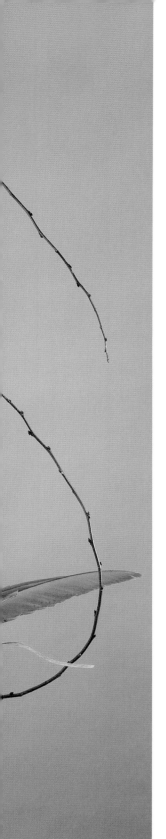

Smoldering elements

in this prairie fire-inspired composition
include roses, rose hips, privet berries,
pepperberries, sycamore leaves,
microbloom waxflowers and deer antlers.

DESIGN TIP In both color and texture,
the antlers in this design act as extensions
of the urn, providing free-form handles to
an otherwise classic-shaped vessel.

This modern version of a Victorian
epergne—the antique of which might
have been hand-carried by early settlers
to the heartland — holds Indian corn, faux pheasant
feathers, grains and assorted dried materials as well as fresh
amaryllises, 'Kardinal' roses, artichokes, *Ranunculuses*, parrot
tulips, Christmas bush, *Leucadendrons*, rose hips, red dogwood
branches and *Magnolia* leaves.

DESIGN TIP Notice how the fresh materials, which require
water, are placed into the central vase while dried and permanent botanicals are placed into the outer compartment, creating a visually interesting potpourri of color and texture.

With his Scottish heritage in mind, Bill chose these tartans for their earthy hues. Clusters of fresh roses and dried poppy pods, which anchor the design, are surrounded by swirling sparks of color from fresh rose hips and evergreens. The shed antler of the prairie's native deer accents the fabric wrap.

DESIGN TIP Wrapping a vase in a textile offers limitless options for easily sourced choices in color, pattern, texture and motif.

Contained in a crackle-finish vase resembling vintage ironstone, **a pairing of leeks towers triumphantly over this winter-white collection** of 'Virginia' roses, ornamental kale, microbloom waxflowers, birch bark, artichokes, privet berries, sycamore leaves and burgundy-leafed ivy.

DESIGN TIP Accents to a design, like the coordinating leek and the novel introduction of a cauliflower head at the base of the container, extend compositions beyond their expected borders, furnishing a decorative setting.

Poppy pods, eggplants, heirloom squashes
with a verdigris finish from Bill's garden, and
a delicate wreath fashioned
from vines add distinction
to a collection of winter-white botanicals
featured in this mounded urn.

DESIGN TIP To create greater depth in a shallow bowl
while avoiding an overstuffed look, arrange the chunkier
elements, like the squashes and eggplants, around a smaller
container, filled with floral foam, that is hidden in the center.

Before plants can survive on the prairie, they must put down deep roots, so their vitality relies on what is protected underground. Here, a collection of spring plants, fragile in their shallow container garden, **peek out into the elements but stay close to the ground, hoping to survive any adverse conditions.** An ornamental kale, Ranunculus blossoms and buds, Bouvardias, Lysimachias, lamb's-ears foliage, variegated lily grass and branches compose the faux planting.

DESIGN TIP When choosing elements for a design, save the flower buds rather than discard them. As seen here, they can create great interest, especially when arranged in groups.

85

"Difficult to categorize yet easy to recognize, it's the excitement of **something new** that makes design modern."

The idea of "modern" is a concept that dates itself almost as quickly as it is defined. At one moment, it is the latest thing, then suddenly it becomes retrospective. Modern design opens the floodgate for individual interpretation and expressionism. Terms like eclectic, abstract, sculptural, free form, contemporary and geometric sound right, but they have ties to the past, and modern design always pushes us toward the future. So maybe it's about daring to experiment; reaching for what best represents tomorrow; and, ultimately, allowing nature to prove, once again, it beat us to the punch.

MODERN

Dynamic line and implied motion are two characteristics that Bill finds present in any design he describes as modern. Here, displayed above Bill's collection of glass pitchers, the interplay of two strong-lined materials — fasciated willows and callas — compete for attention while anchored at their binding point with calla foliage and Viburnum blossoms.

The youthful among us seem to gravitate most readily to the modern aesthetic, and contemporary floral jewelry is a growing trend with nuptial and prom flowers. Here,

a fashion-forward choker makes an abstract statement

with bits and pieces of 'Mambo' spray roses, a Gerbera and miniature Cymbidium orchids assembled with the aid of aluminum and bullion wire.

DESIGN TIP   To create long-lasting floral jewelry, always choose flowers and foliages that maintain their form out of water. Fresh materials also can be sprayed with an antitranspirant, which slows dehydration.

Modern graphics on decorative papers set the tone for this **ethnic-inspired assemblage.** Swags and loops of aluminum wire and a garland of red *Hypericum* berries create interest in dueling floral clusters featuring *Gerberas*, *Anthuriums*, Iceland poppies and bear grass.

DESIGN TIP Prior to placing flowers in the vases, Bill arranged these small clusters in his hand and secured them with a wrapping of decorative wire.

89

Regimented rows of 'Granny Smith' apples and salal leaves stand at attention in a square plastic tray that is surfaced in salal leaves. Hypericum berries and tufts of Viburnum blooms fill the gaps between the fruit and foliage. Dynamic lines of playful lily grass disrupt the order.

Blurring the distinction between modern and garden styling,

Bill employs fragrant lemons to elevate the diminutive blossoms of spray roses. Bittersweet vines and lily grass intersect abstractly while four cylinder vases are contained in one of Bill's signature foliage-covered trays.

DESIGN TIP Although designed for round or square tables, this composition can be reconfigured for rectangular or oval tables by rearranging the auxiliary elements, which include ball-shaped candles and short cylinders that hold floating candles and lily-grass clippings.

This "sculpture" of metal accessories and *Anthurium* blossoms is at once simple and complex. While the elements are as minimal as the design, the impact is powerful and strong. Bill calls this contemporary expression **one of the purist forms of modern— where each element is distinguished, yet all work together as one.**

DESIGN TIP Not all art vessels are watertight. If the opening of a container is too small to accommodate a liner, and when only a few stems of flowers are needed to complete the arrangement, place individual flower stems into plastic water tubes, and drop them into the container(s).

Showcasing a single type of flower is the essence of this styling, which is known as "monobotanical design." Here, the emphasis is less about the arrangement of flowers and more about the *Gerberas* as graphic elements. Short pieces of chopped steel grass decorate the interiors of the square glass vases while, in the tall vase, longer blades create intersecting lines that are randomly accented with plastic beads sourced at any craft store.

DESIGN TIP Choose beads with small openings, so they will stay secure when threaded onto the grass.

Eclectic — a buzzword for seemingly random but artful collections — aptly describes the materials in these component pieces. They have no relationship except their color. It's the tension between these unrelated elements that creates excitement. Contemporary glass cylinders, tropical *Anthuriums*, garden *Ranunculuses*, Christmas ornaments and metallic wire compose the stylish array of misfits.

DESIGN TIP To secure the Christmas ornaments into the vases, hot-glue a wood pick or stake into the opening of each ornament to create a "stem" that can be inserted into the containers.

95

With all their graphic impact, including ethnic-inspired beading, bold pattern and intricate detailing, these designs provide a modern take on traditional bud-vase arrangements. 'Versilia' roses, miniature callas, croton leaves and lily grass make up the guestlist of this not-your-normal pair of vases.

DESIGN TIP To add beads to the center of a rose, thread beads onto a short piece of wire bent in a hairpin shape, then insert the ends of the wire into the rose's center.

Architecturally arranged, these component designs are an industrial revolution of ordered placements, including manicured rows of stacked salal leaves, colorful Gerberas, fuzzy Dianthuses and pea gravel punctuated with sweeping lines of lily grass and poppy pods. The rooftop garden of an urban loft was Bill's inspiration for this dynamic duo.

DESIGN TIP When creating component designs, remember that repeating dynamic lines, like the ones achieved here with lily grass, can visually connect the designs, increasing their compatibility.

the snowy branches reflected in the decorative vases are repeated in the styling elements, establishing a patterned setting for these minimal placements of *Phalaenopsis* orchids.

DESIGN TIP   Look for vases with patterns, shapes and motifs that can be repeated with botanical materials in the composition.

Geometry adds a modern accent to these floating *Phalaenopsis* blossoms. Plastic rings and decorative beads threaded onto a wood skewer seem high-tech as they mimic patterns inspired by computer chips.

DESIGN TIP A walk through a craft outlet or hardware store can reveal endless options for items that can be repurposed for floral design.

The green elements in this design come in
botanical waves of layered salal leaves,
arching lily grass and two varieties of bubbly chrysanthemums — button and spider — which echo the bubblelike iridescent beading. Long-lasting button mums extend the design beyond the container, adding intriguing accents to a setting that would best serve as event décor.

DESIGN TIP   When choosing a flower to use as an out-of-water accent, favor varieties like these button mums that will last for hours before showing signs of wilting.

This composition exhibits all the **characteristics that define formal-linear floral design.** Well-organized materials are arranged in distinct groups, with strong lines and bold forms. The color theme is green and more green, combining *Ranunculuses*, *Hypericum*, *Dianthuses*, lily grass, and salal and geranium leaves. A tall partner design combines layered placements of salal with a circlet of *Hypericum* berries.

DESIGN TIP   Bill alternated a few electric-green geranium leaves between the stacks of deep-green salal leaves, advising: "When using only one color in a design, look for ways to contrast light and dark values for added visual interest."

When designing in clear glass, Bill pays as much attention to the arrangement of elements that are "under glass" as he does to those that emerge from the container.

Hot-pink sticks and skeletonized *Magnolia* leaves combine with fresh tulips, roses and *Gerberas* to create abstract compositions in which the intersecting lines and layered materials are showcased in the clear glass vessels.

DESIGN TIP The skeletonized *Magnolia* leaf is adhered to the exterior of the vase with double-sided photo-mounting tape.

Grouped placements of floral materials are common in professionally designed arrangements, yet the technique of clustering elements retains a modern feel. The segregated materials in this romantic heart include spray roses, waxflowers, *Limonium* and variegated English boxwood.

DESIGN TIP This heart-shaped composition is created in a miniature floral-foam heart form; however, a thin piece of floral foam scored with a heart-shaped cookie cutter would also work nicely.

Sometimes flowers are crafted into completely new and unexpected forms, taken beyond the natural into abstractions that break all the rules. Such is the case with this vase arrangement that features an armature, created with calla stems, that supports the excitingly disjointed placements of miniature callas, Gerberas, carnations and tulips.

DESIGN TIP Using leftover lengths of stems, such as the miniature calla stems in this arrangement, to create an armature that supports the florals also adds artistic value to designs and reduces waste by creatively incorporating all flower parts.

Bill identifies movement as one of the hallmarks of modern styling. Here, the repetition of circular lines — in both the flowers and the decorative aluminum wires — harmonizes with the painted surface on which the arrangement is placed, creating the illusion that all are swirling in the same direction. The floral mix comprises ornamental kale, hyacinths, miniature callas and *Gerberas*.

DESIGN TIP The variations in height and depth among the floral groupings, and the dimension those variations achieve, promote a feeling of movement as the eyes travel up and down and around the groupings.

These *Cymbidium* orchids seem perfectly positioned
for entertaining. The central glass container features an
intersecting framework of golden-
twig dogwood branches and lily grass,
on which the orchids are displayed. Bubble-shaped
glass satellites extend the decoration, making party-
table adornment a perfect application for this design.

DESIGN TIP   The foliage discs on which the orchids
rest are created by covering cardboard circles with *Galax*
leaves. The leaves are secured with spray floral adhesive.

Painted dried materials, including panchu springs, wood string and bits of buri tips, create **art under glass.** By using only a single hue, Bill simplifies the composition so that viewers' attention focuses on the interesting twists and turns the materials create as well as the purposeful variations of texture and proportion.

DESIGN TIP Many dried materials become more pliable when soaked in water; however, test a small piece of a material to see if it is colorfast before soaking an entire bunch.

Alive with texture, this eclectic mix of pincushions, 'Charlotte' roses, *Hypericum* and bird's-nest-fern fronds sports an organic, grass-covered heart, which is suspended from a rustic garland made of birch twigs and copper wire that encircles the vase.

DESIGN TIP To create the heart, glue blades of lily grass diagonally onto a cardboard heart with waterproof floral adhesive, then trim the edges of the grass to shape.

Bill finds that, in nature, it's common for beauty to emerge from chaos. This 21st-century symphony of crisscrossing lines, created with chopped willow twigs, serves as a complex background upon which the distinctive beauty of a single *Anthurium* is showcased.

DESIGN TIP The garland of *Hypericum* berries is created by threading the fruit lengthwise onto a sturdy but flexible wire.

FLORISTS' REVIEW

President: Frances Dudley, AAF
Publisher: Talmage McLaurin, AIFD
Floral Designer: Bill Harper, AIFD, AAF, FAM
Author: Talmage McLaurin, AIFD
Copy Editors: David L. Coake, Shelley Urban
Photographers: Stephen Smith, Mark Robbins
Creative Coordinator: James Miller, AIFD
Art Director: Holly Cott

Cover photo and photos on Pages 2, 3, 6-7, 11, 16, 23, 37, 58-59, 87-88 and 111 by Mark Robbins.

All other photos by Stephen Smith.

Nature Takes Over: The Designs of Bill Harper was produced by Florists' Review Enterprises, Inc., Topeka, Kansas; www.floristsreview.com.

Printed in China by Regent Publishing Services Limited Shau Kei Wan, Hong Kong

ISBN: 978-0-9801815-2-4

Florists' Review Enterprises is the leading magazine and book publishing company for the U.S. floral industry. The company is home to Florists' Review and Super Floral Retailing magazines as well as to Florists' Review Bookstore, the industry's premier marketplace for books and other educational materials.